The Simple Way
Tarny

The Simple Way To Get Motivated

© Copyright Tarnya Coley 2020
Published by Tarnya Coley Publishing LTD

All rights reserved 2020 Tarnya Coley Publishing LTD

Dedication

To my lovely husband & children

This book is for you if:

- You are looking for a simple but effective way to get motivated

- You need encouraging and uplifting words for yourself and others

- You need to be inspired

- You need a kick start to your day

Introduction

The Simple Way To Get Motivated is a motivational book which leaves the reader empowered to take charge of their mindset.

This book was written to inspire and change the way you view situations.

The words in this book are encouraging and uplifting words to make you feel motivated and get a spring in your step!

'A positive thought, a word a day, helps to keep the negativity at bay!'

The Simple Way To Get Motivated is a continuation of Chapter 12 in my best-selling book *Open Doors.*

POWER OF WORDS

1

AUTHENTIC

Just be YOU! Don't fake it.
You are unique. Embrace it.

2

ATTITUDE

Let your positive attitude
radiate and shine through!
Let it be contagious.

3

ASSERTIVE

Today is going to be a great day.
Be confident and bold.

4

ACHIEVEMENT

I will achieve what I set out to do today.
At the end of the day I will reflect on what I have
achieved and celebrate.

5
ALIVE
I'm alive! I'm breathing.
Be happy!

6
ADVENTURE
Life is one big adventure!
Learn to navigate your way through.

7
ACCEPT
Do not allow the negative
opinion of others to change you.

8

APPEARANCE

Be ready for every occasion.
Even when you don't feel like it.

9

ACCOMPLISHED

Have a winning attitude. You will accomplish the
goals that you have set yourself.

10

ADAPT

Same old thinking - same old results. Adapt the
plan and you will get a different outcome.

11

AMBITION

Don't settle for mediocre.
Go for it!

12

AWESOME

Do not let fear stop you from being the awesome person you were created to be!

13

ANTICIPATION

Something good is about to happen!

14

ASPIRATION

Aim high. Set your goals and do it!

15
ACT
Do something each day towards your goals.

16
AMAZING
Tell yourself each morning,
'I am AMAZING!'
Tell someone else today that *they* are 'amazing!'

17
ACCOUNTABLE
Share with someone all about your wins and your
challenges.

18
ASCEND
Keep on climbing. Don't stop, you can do this!

19
ACTIVATE
Activate your purpose and do what you are *purposed* to do.

20
AIM HIGH
Take the limits off. You will never know what you are capable of if you do not go for it!

21
ATTEMPT
Have a go! Try something new. You'll surprise yourself.

22

ACTION

Action what you set out to do.
Don't just say it.

23

ABUNDANCE

There is so much to be thankful for!
Take the time to reflect.

24

AWARE

Be careful of the negative self-doubt.
Don't second guess yourself.

25

AFFIRM

Promise yourself that you will do the
best you can.

26
ADMIRE
Be proud of what you have achieved!

27
AGREE
Do not agree with the negative words that have ever been spoken to you.

28
ARISE
It is your time to arise and shine and do what you are purposed to do.

29
BELONGING
Do not let others make you feel that you do not fit in.

30
BEAMING
Continue to shine like the star you are!

31
BEAUTY
See the beauty all around you!
Look in the mirror and say,
'I am beautiful!'

32
BLESSED
Appreciate what you have.
Count your blessings.

33
BIG HEART
Be kind & generous. Have the right motive.

34
BRAVE
Tell yourself this IS possible!

35
BLOOM
Flourish in every situation.
You were born to succeed!

36
BEYOND
Go beyond average and do more than expected!

37
BREATHTAKING
Continue to do things that take someone's breath away!

38
BALANCED
Balance is the key to take control of your life.

39
BENEFITS
What I set out to do today, is it beneficial?
Stay focused!

40
BE TRUE
Be you!
Don't ever try to be something you're not.

41
BOLD
Be fearless and stand firm.

42
BUILD
Build positive character that will last.

43
BEYOND
Go beyond average and do more than expected!

44
BOLD
Do not stand in the shadows.
Stand up and be counted!

45
BE BETTER
Be the better person!
Do not lower your standards.

46
BE FULFILLED
Be happy in what you are doing.
Make it count.

47
BLISS
Enjoy the company of others.
Hangout with like-minded people.

48
BUBBLY
Be full of life, not strife!

49
BRILLIANT
Do something that will make you proud.

50
BOUNDARY
Ensure you have limits.
Don't allow others to cross the line.

51
COURAGEOUS
Have a courageous heart.
Be brave!

52
CHARACTER
Have a positive attitude!
Character check.
'Check yo'self before you wreck yo'self!'

53
CHERISH
Cherish what you have and
take pleasure in it.

54
CLARITY
Whatever you do, make sure you are clear on
why you are doing it.

55
CALM
Stay calm in every situation.
Do not act on your emotions.

56
CHANGE
Your circumstances will not always be the same.
Believe this in your heart right now and watch
how change WILL come!

57
CELEBRATE
Always celebrate your wins.
It doesn't matter how big or small.
Have a party of one!

58
CHAMPION
Speak positive to yourself. I AM A CHAMPION!
You will start to feel and act differently when you
change the way you talk.

59
CONNECTED
Connect with like-minded people so that you can
build each other up!

60
CONTENT
Be happy with what you have been blessed with.

61
CARING
Take care of yourself and others.

62
CAPABLE
Do not talk yourself out of it.
You can do it!

63
CHOICE
Do what is right and make the right choice.

64

CHALLENGE

Embrace the challenges and learn from them. It's all part of the journey.

65

CONQUER

Rise & conquer!
You *can* defeat those obstacles!
You *will* triumph!

66

COMMITTED

Stick at it!
Follow through and complete the task.

67

CREATIVE

Be resourceful.
You are more creative than you think.

68
CONFIDENCE
Stand up for what you believe in and stick to your principles.

69
CAPACITY
You can always do more!
You have the ability to do it!

70
CHARMING
Be pleasant to others.

71
COMPLETE
Be a person that finishes things.

72
COMPETITION
You are not in competition with others.
We are all on different parts of our journey.

73
CALLED
Only *you* can do what *you* were called to do, in a
way that only *you* can do it!

74
CONFIDENCE
Be bold and fearless!

75
CAN DO
Have a *CAN DO* attitude!
Believe in yourself!

76
COMPASSION
Put yourself in other people's shoes.
Do not judge.

77
CERTAIN
Be assured in your endeavours.
Don't waiver.

78
CLASSIC
You are one of a kind!

79
COOL
Keep a cool head. Don't blow it.

80
CAPTAIN
You are the captain of your journey.
Take charge!

81
DETERMINATION
Have that fighting spirit that nothing is going to
stop you from fulfilling your goals!

82
DIGNITY
Know who you are and respect yourself.

83
DELIGHT
Being pleasant is a choice.
Make the right choice.

84
DESIRE
Have aspirations!
This will give you focus on your journey.

85
DAZZLED
Dazzle someone today with your smile & your beauty!

86
DREAM BIG
Take the limits off and dare to dream.
Dreams do come true.

87
DEDICATE
Whatever you do today be devoted in what you are doing.

88
DISCIPLINE
Be well organised!
This will help you to be laser focused.

89
DIRECTION
Staying on the right path will help to keep
moving forward.

90
DIFFERENCE
Make a positive difference in someone else's life!

91
DESERVE
You should have the best!

92
DESTINY
Your future is great! Just believe it!

93
DEVELOPMENT
Always find a way to invest in yourself.
You are worth investing in.

94
DISTINGUISHED
Be dignified and noble.

95
DIVINE
Create happy moments!

___96___

EACH DAY COUNT YOUR BLESSINGS

Look at what you have, and you will surprise
yourself!

___97___

ENCOURAGE

Encourage someone today!
You never know just how much they may need it!

___98___

EMBRACE

Embrace the high and the lows.
It is how you look at your situation.

99
ENRICH
Live a meaningful life!

100
EXCITED
Step into your day!
Be ecstatic about the changes you can make!

101
ENERGY
Throw your energy at what you are doing!

102
EARNEST
Have that conviction.
Be serious in what you are doing.

103

ENJOY

Live life to the full! Enjoy every moment!

104

ENGAGE

Get involved and participate.
Make those connections.

105

EDUCATE

Learning never stops!

106
EXCELLENCE
In everything you do, do it with excellence!

107
ENTHUSIASTIC
Approach the day with enthusiasm!
It will change your whole outlook!

108
ELEVATE
Lift others up. We all need a helping hand!

109
EFFECTIVE
Today is the day that you decide that in
everything, you will show up and be efficient!

110

ESTABLISH
Create memories and set a routine.

111

EXPAND
Increase in your knowledge.
This will help you to develop.

112

EXCEL
Whatever you are doing,
do it well!

113
EXHALE
Remember to take time out to recharge.

114
ENLIGHTEN
Enlighten someone with your knowledge. Make an impact in someone's life.

115
ELIMINATE EXCUSES
NO more excuses.
Just get the job done!

116
EFFORTLESS
When you are operating in your gifts, you will make it look graceful.

117

ESSENTIAL

Make time for you!
Your needs are important.

118

ELECTRIFYING

Be thrilled with excitement!
Today is going to be a good day!

119

FEARLESS

Go get it! Be unafraid!

120
FOCUS
When you focus it reduces the distractions, so stay focused!

121
FRIENDSHIP
Appreciate your friends!
Value the people in have in your life.

122
FAITH
Have faith in what you want to see happen.
It will happen!

123
FLOURISH
Do well in whatever task you are doing.

124
FREEDOM
Do not let your circumstances hold you back. You are not restricted.

125
FIXATED
Be absorbed in what you set out to do.

126
FASCINATING
Do something interesting today!
Take up a new hobby.

127
FORWARD
Don't look back.
Focus on what is ahead.

128
FABULOUS
Remember you are fabulous!

129
FUNNY
Look at the funny side.
Don't take yourself too seriously.

130
FRIENDLY
Be the person that extends a hand of friendship.

131
FANTASTIC
Today is going to be a fantastic day!

132
FAMILIAR
Recognise your strengths.

133
GENUINE
Be real & authentic!

134
GRATITUDE
Show your appreciation for someone today.
Tell them you are grateful for them.

135
GRACEFUL
Be charming & pleasant.
You will feel so much better!

136
GLOWING
Wherever you go today, be the person that lights
up the room!

137
GIVER
Give someone your time today.

138
GUIDE
Show someone the right way.
Point them in the right direction.

139
GROWTH
Nothing grows in comfort zones.

140
GOALS
Set goals. Write them down. Action them!

141
GIFT
Life is a gift, handle it with care.

142
GREAT
Great things are going happen!
Have a mindset shift.

143
GENIUS
You are intelligent and smart.
Don't ever let anyone tell you otherwise.

144
GROUNDED
Stand firm and believe!
Do not compromise.

145

GREATNESS

Live life on a new level!
Step into your greatness!

146

GAME CHANGER

Change the game!
No more business as usual!

147

GET UP

Don't stay down.
It's time to get up and move from where you are at.

148
GIVE BACK
Freely give to others.
Not because you have to, but because you want to!

149
GENEROUS
Be generous and don't hold back.

150
GOOD
See the good in others!

151
HANDY
What skills do you have?
Use them and be effective.

152
HARMONY
Be of one accord.
Great things happen when you are unified!

153
HONOURABLE
In all that you do ensure that it is upright.

154
HOPE
Expect it to happen.
Do not give up!

155
HELPING-HAND
Help others up.
Be the one that shows kindness.

156
HARVEST
It's time to reap what you have sown!

157
HAPPY
Focus on what you have and be happy.

158
HARD WORK
You must put in the hard work so you can get
positive results!

159
HEALTHY
To keep a healthy mind,
feed yourself on positivity!

160
HONEST
Just be real!

161
HEALING
Allow yourself to be healed from your past, so you
can move forward successfully into a glorious
future.

162
INSPIRE
Lead the way and be an inspiration!
You never know who's watching.

163
IGNITE
Do what you love to do!
Do not let your desires die.

164
INCREDIBLE
Shine like the star you are!
You are incredible!

165
I BELIEVE I CAN
Have a positive attitude and know that you **CAN**
do it!

166
INTEGRITY
Be the person that wherever you show up, you are being yourself.

167
I AM
Speak words of affirmation, not elimination.

168
IMPROVE
Remember you *can* make improvements. You are a work in progress.

169
INFLUENCE
Be a positive influencer!
Make a change in other people's lives.

170
IMPORTANT
Make room for what is important.
Don't ignore it.

171
IMPORTANT
You are significant!

172
IMPACT
Your purpose and plan should make a positive
impact.

173
I CAN
Have a 'can do' attitude!

174
INNOVATIVE
Without vision there is no discipline.

175
INSTANTANEOUS
Respond immediately. Do not delay!

176
IDEAL
There is no 'ideal' moment.
Do it now!

177
JOY
Take joy in what you are doing.
It makes the process more enjoyable.

178
JOVIAL
Be that fun-loving person!

179
JOLLY
Be jolly and enjoy life!

180
KIND
Be the person that shows kindness.

181
KNOW YOUR WORTH
You are significant!
Don't ever put yourself down.

182
KEEN
Be enthusiastic!
It changes the whole mood!

183
KEY
The key to moving forward is to keep moving forward.

184
LOVE
Love yourself and love others.

185
LIFE- LONG LEARNER
Invest in yourself.
You are worth investing in!

186
LIGHT
Wherever you go the room lights up because YOU are there!

187

LET GO!

There are some things that you need to get rid of
so you can become the person you should be.

188

LEADER

Lead the way!
You don't know who you could be inspiring.

189

LEVEL UP

Don't stay at the same level.
Challenge yourself and progress to the *next* level.

190
LION
Be strong and courageous!

191
LIFE IS PRECIOUS
Don't take life for granted.

192
LIFE IS A JIGSAW
Life has millions of jigsaw pieces.
You just have to figure it out.

193
LIFT UP
Be the type of person that lifts others up, not
treads upon them.

194
LEARNING
Always be prepared to learn something new!
Knowledge is power.

195
LIVE LIFE
Have a plan for your life.
This will help to clarify your priorities.

196
LAUGH
Laugh a lot. It is good medicine.

197
LEGEND
You are simply awesome.

198
MOVING FORWARD
Standing still is not an option.
Keep taking one step at a time.

199
MOTIVATE
Encourage yourself and encourage others.

200
MISSION
You are on a mission.
You have been given various takes to complete.

201
MIND BLOWING
Don't give up on your dream. It will blow you away when you see your dream comes true.

202
MODIFY
If what you are doing isn't working, adjust the plan.

203
MASTER
Master your mind-set.
Be cautious what you feed it.

204
MINDSET
Shift your focus.
Have a positive mindset.

205
MISSION POSSIBLE
Even when it seems difficult, remember the
mission is possible.

206
MEANINGFUL
Set yourself significant goals.

207
MARVELLOUS
You are absolutely stunning.

208
MERIT
You are a person of true worth.

209
NEVER QUIT
Quitting is easy, pressing in is hard, but worth it.

210
NO LIMITS
The only limit is you!
Take the limits off!

211
OVERCOME
Do not let your situation dictate to you.
You will get through it.

212
OPTIMISTIC
Be *positive* and change your perspective!

213
OPEN
Be open to change, if change is necessary.

214
ON TOP
Keep climbing and don't stop!

215
ONE
There is power in numbers so don't go through your situations alone.

216
OPPORTUNITY
Create moments where you can seize opportunities.

217
ORGANISE
Plan what you are doing.
Have a to do list.

218
OUTSTANDING
Be exceptional in what you are doing.
Set the standard.

219
OPTION
You will always be presented with options. Select
the right one.

220
OWNERSHIP
Take responsibility for your actions.

221
PROMISE
Promise yourself that you will action what you set
out to do.

222
POSITION
Align yourself for success!

223
PLANS
Have a plan for your life.
This will keep you focused and give you direction.

224
PERVERANCE
Know that you have strength inside of you to keep going.

225
PRODUCTIVE
Whatever you do, make sure it brings good results.

226
POTENTIAL
You have the potential to be great!
You have it inside you.

227
POSITIVITY
Positive energy is contagious!

228
PROGRESS
Life is about making progress.
Small steps every day is development.

229
PATIENT
Be tolerate of others.

230
PRIORITY
Prioritise the things that are important.
Make the time.

231
PEACE
Be the peacemaker even in difficult situations.

232
PASSIONATE
Get excited about what you are doing.

233
POWER OF WORDS
Your words are powerful.
Speak life!

234
PLENTIFUL
You have been given so much.
Be thankful!

235
POWER
Take control and take charge of your life!

236
PREPARE
Always put in order what you need.
Be prepared.

237
PRODUCTIVE
Make sure your day is a day filled with action!

238
PERSISTANT
Believe that you can achieve anything!
Keep going!

239
PERFECT
No one is perfect.
Be the best you can be!

240
PRESERVE
Take care of yourself.
Your wellbeing is important.

241
PROACTIVE
Being proactive produces result!

242
POSSIBLE
It *is* possible!
Shift your focus.

243
POSITIVE WORDS
Choose to speak positive words that lift you and others.

244
PAY IT FORWARD
Repay a good deed to someone.

245
PRAISE
Compliment someone today.
Go ahead and make their day!

246
PRACTICAL STEPS
Don't jump in head-first.
Take a step back and take realistic steps.

247
POSITIVE VIBES ONLY
Give off the right vibes.

248
PRICELESS
You are invaluable!

249
PREPERATION
Always prepare with excellence.

250
PURPOSE
Your life has purpose and value.

251
PROPEL
Push forward and keep going!

252
PHENOMENAL
You are remarkable!

253
PLEASURE
Take pleasure in serving others.

254
PLEASANT
Be mindful how you treat others.

255
QUIET TIME
Have some 'ME' time.
You are important.

256
QUALITY
Whatever you do, do it with style and grace.

257
QUICK
Be quick to listen and be careful how you respond.

258
RESILIENT
You *can* bounce back!
You have the inner strength.

259
RESPECT
Know your worth!

260
RENEW
Positive thinking helps you to focus.

261
REMEMBER
Never forget your purpose and why you do what you do.

262
REMARKABLE
Be extraordinary!

263
REJUVENATE
Take time out and be refreshed.

264
RADIANT
You were born to shine!

265
RELISH
Enjoy the process and learn from what you are going through.

266
RANDOM ACTS OF KINDNESS
Do something nice for someone. No agenda. Don't tweet it. Just do it!

267
REWARD
When you have achieved a milestone, have a party of one!

268
RELAX
Stop rushing around.
Stop and pause.

269
RESTORE
Bring back the passion you had to smash those goals.

270
REACH OUT
Be a helping hand to someone. There is always someone who needs support.

271
RESULTS
Change the way you do things.
It will bring positive results.

272
READY, SET, GO
Take action to make your dream come true!

273
REQUIREMENTS
What do I need to do to make it happen?

274
REVELATION
Write down your eye-opening thoughts.

275
RELIABLE
Be a reliable friend that others can depend on.

276
REVITALISE
Reflect, reboot and refresh yourself.

277
REFRESH
Refresh yourself, take a step back and refocus.

278
RISE UP
It is your time. Do not let the negative stop you!

279
RENOWED
Be renowned for excellence in all you do.

280
RADICAL
Set your foundation and be swayed.

281
REFINE
If it isn't working, refine what you are doing.

282
RADIANT
Shine like the star you are!

283
STRENGTH
Remember you have the power to keep on going.

284
SINCERE
Do not be fake. Be truthful.

285
SPARKLING
Smile and sparkle!

286
SYNCHRONISED
Do not get anxious.

287
SUCCESS
True success is happiness.

288
STRIVE
Do your best because that's all that is required.

289
SELF-WORTH
Do not allow the negative opinion of
others to change you.

290
SUPPORTIVE
Support others.
There is always someone who will need your
help.

291
SET YOUR FOUNDATION
Once you have established who you are, no one
can rock you!

292
SORT IT
Be organised and stay ahead of the journey.

293
SATISFACTION
In whatever you do, have a sense of contentment.
Know that you have done well!

294
SHARING IS CARING
Show someone that you love them by carrying out
a nice deed.

295
SPARKLE & SHINE
Keep on showing up!

296
SELF-DISCIPLINE
In order to complete your tasks and take action,
you have to have strength of mind.

297
SIMPLE
Don't over complicate things.
Keep it simple.

298
SHOW UP
Have a positive attitude and be laser focused.

299
SOWING SEEDS
Sow positive seeds in your mind and watch them grow.

300
SCOPE
There are so many possibilities!
Take the limits off!

301
SECOND TO NONE
You are great! One of a kind!

302
SHARP
Stay sharp and driven minded.

303
SEASONS
Flourish in your season.

304
SKILLS
Use your skills and you will get better at what you do.

305
SOLUTION
Be the person who finds the solution.

306
STEPPING OUT
When you step out of your comfort zone, you will surprise yourself at what you can do!

307
SELF-ESTEEM
Positive self-talk is important to boost your self-esteem.

308
TRANSFORMATION
Transformation is a process, a lasting positive change.

309
THANKFUL
Everyday think of something to be thankful for.

310
THOUGHTFUL
Consider the needs of others throughout your day.

311
THRIVE
Flourish today! Don't just survive.

312
TRANQUIL
Make time during your week to relax and recharge.

313
TRUST
Have the confidence to know that you have the
power to do anything!

314
TIME OUT
Schedule in a break.
It doesn't matter how long.

315
TEAM WORK
Working together can help you to get the job
completed in a shorter space of time.

316
TALENT
You have the ability!
Prove to yourself you can!

317
TRIUMPHANT
You are a conqueror!

318
TRY
If you don't try it, you will never know that you can
do it.

319
THINK BIG
Don't be afraid to *think big*!
Break through those limitations!

320

TEACHABLE

Be teachable.
There is always something to learn.

321

TRANSMIT

What are you transmitting through the messages
you send each day?

322

TRANSPARENT

Be clear on what you set out to do.

323
TAKE RISKS
When you take risks, you are driven to learn new skills.

324
THROUGH IT
Go through the process. It's part of the journey.

325
TENDER
Be compassionate and kind.

326
THOROUGH
Be thoroughly prepared in what you need to do.

327
THRILLED
Be happy! Think on the good things.

328
TENACITY
Be determined in pursuing your goals!

329
TESTIMONY
You have to go through your test, then you can share with others how you overcame.

330
TIDY
De-clutter and get organised.

331
TEAM
Being part of a team builds trust.
You need others around you.

332
TEACH
Inspire others with what you know.

333
UPBEAT
Be cheerful and chirpy!

334
UNAFRAID
Be free from fear.

335
UNIQUE
You don't have to be like
everyone else. Be YOU!

336
UNDERSTANDING
Take the time to understand.
You will have a better perspective.

337

UPLIFTING

Inspire someone with some positive words.

338

UNSTOPPABLE

Be relentless in your endeavours!

339

UPBEAT

Change your perspective and be positive!

340

VALUE

Know your worth!

341
VENTURE
Try something new!

342
VISUALISE
Place your dream at the for
front of your mind.

343
VICTORY
You can do it!

344
VIBRANT
Re-energise yourself!

345
VISION
Create a vision for your life.
This will give you clarity.

346
VIP
You are important! Know your worth!

347
VALID
Keep dreaming! Your dreams are valid.

348
VIRTUE
Be a person of high moral standards.

349
WISDOM
Have the wisdom in knowing when to speak up.

350
WOW
Wise Optimistic Words
Change your language and speak positively!

351
WONDERFUL
Something wonderful is going to happen!

352
WINNER
Have a *winner* mentality!
It will change your outlook.

353
WONDER
Don't wonder what will happen.
Make it happen!

354
WISE
You are wiser than you think.

355
WARM THOUGHTS
Encourage yourself. It will lift you up.

356
WILL POWER
This will boost the strength you need to complete
your daily tasks.

357
WILLING
Be willing to go the extra mile.

358
WATCHFUL
Be careful who you have around you.

359
WELL DONE
Appreciate someone today!

360
WELCOME
Be welcoming and accommodating.

361
WELL
Live *well* and prosper!

362
YES
Get rid of fear! Yes, you can do it!

363
ZEST
Live life with excitement and anticipation!

364
ZEAL
Be passionate!

365
YOU ARE A TREASURE
Terrific
Resilient
Enjoyable
Amazing
Selfless
Unique
Reliable
Encouraging

Message for you

Remember the Power Of Words. Our words have the power to lift yourself and others.
Speak life to yourself and those around you. When you do, situations change.

Tarnya Coley

Email
tarnya@ibelieveican.co.uk

Website
www.ibelieveican.co.uk

Instagram
https://www.instagram.com/teacoley/

LinkedIn
https://www.linkedin.com/in/tarnya-coley/